HOW TO MAKE MONEY IN THE MODERN WORLD

The Gig Economy and Beyond

Mauricio Rubio

YESI EDUCATION
Visit our website at www.yesieducation.com

CONTENTS

INTRODUCTION

Humanity has come a long way, and we live in exciting times. Truly remarkable times. Times of opportunity at your fingertips. Never before in human history has it been so easy to make so much money, so fast, with little to no investment. Never.

Think about it. Transport yourself 100 years ago or not even that far, just a few decades ago before the time of the internet, apps and smartphones. If you wanted to setup shop, you were bound and constrained by the physical limits of time, space and location. All constraints unknown to the digital world, the modern world.

In this world, you can potentially target thousands, well millions and even billions of people at the same time with the same product or service. There are no physical boundaries or constraints and you can even sell in different time zones, locations and channels in less than a blink of an eye. It is incredible and something that has transformed humanity and the way we interact in ways few truly understand. Especially if you didn't even see or experience what we "had" before.

It's in this context and under this circumstances that the Gig Economy and Beyond is born. And we will cover the key concepts and things you need to consider as well as different tools, products or services that will allow you to leverage on what this modern world offers to make money, build wealth and perhaps even pursue some of your deepest passions in unconventional ways without the shackles of a traditional day to day, nine to five job.

The world has changed, and opportunities abound. But you might not even be aware of what's around or how to make the most of it. And here's where I come in. I want to demystify the Gig Economy and help you help yourself to a piece of the pie.

Whatever happens and whether you decide to pursue this or not, know this: if you're not part of the gig economy, you are paying for it.

CHAPTER 1: WHAT IS THE GIG ECONOMY?

The Gig Economy refers to the informal, casual & independent economy in which people leverage on technology, their possessions or skills to generate revenue. And, in which there's generally no employee-employer relationship as such (at least not in the traditional and conventional sense), but more of a fee for services, royalties or commission for products, content or some form of value that you as an individual provide to a company or others.

Regardless of whether you are conscious of it or not, you are exposed to the gig economy on a regular basis. It is all around you and many have focused on it to develop additional revenue streams and others have gone as far as to make it their primary source of income.

Examples of the Gig economy would be things familiar to you such as Uber, Airbnb and even Youtube, but the reality (unknown to a vast majority of people) is that the

Gig Economy goes way beyond these popular products or services and provides an incredible number of opportunities for those willing to do what must be done to achieve what can be achieved.

CHAPTER 2: WHY JOIN THE GIG ECONOMY?

There are many reasons why you should join the Gig Economy and of course they will vary from person to person, but here are some of the most popular reasons why people join the Gig Economy and choose to make money in unconventional ways:

- To generate additional revenue streams
- To replace their main source of income and perhaps quit their day to day job
- To complement their main source of income
- To have direct control of their schedule and working hours
- Because they get satisfaction from doing something they love
- Because they get to decide whether to accept or not a job, offer or task
- Because it can help them achieve their dreams and goals

- Because they want to explore something new, different and perhaps exciting

CHAPTER 3: CAN ANYONE REALLY JOIN THE GIG ECONOMY?

Yes, anyone can join. But like anything else, it's not a one size fits all approach. What you do will largely depend on your particular situation or context and the skills, assets or intangible benefits you can provide. The good news is that given the Gig Economy is so big and diverse, you will have plenty of options to choose from and I would recommend that you focus on one initially. And one that is particularly in tune with who you are as a person or what you aim to achieve in life. What gives you satisfaction and makes you happy. This will be a key success factor in your journey.

I have seen kids, the young and the old in the Gig Economy. There are truly no limits on this. Some of the apps, tools, products and services might have limitations around age, but a lot of them don't & those that do have sensible and logical limitations around that. Not too different from what you would see anywhere else, on a regular job or startup.

CHAPTER 4: HOW MUCH MONEY CAN I MAKE?

It varies widely. Some people are making a few bucks here and there, others are making hundreds whilst others thousands and some even millions. Obviously, those making millions are the few, not the many. But the point is, you can make a lot of money if you put in the effort, work hard, position yourself as an expert in your field, develop a reputation, social following, etc.

Now, to keep it real and manage expectations, I don't want you to start off thinking that this is a get rich quick scheme or a dodgy line of business. It isn't. And if that's what you were expecting I would suggest that you close this book now and move on to the next thing. But if you want to learn how to make money in the modern world, how to potentially replace your current income or complement it, well then this book will help you. And I will teach you everything I can to help you succeed. Think of what you will learn here as more of a get rich slow process, but more than that I would say that in the end you will reap the benefits if you're persistent and patient. And if you work hard. Yes, I'm sorry to tell you but you will have to work hard and it won't be easy.

On the plus side, if you make the right choice and choose something that you're actually passionate about, it won't feel like a job but more like a hobby and you will enjoy it.

But back to the original question, according to Forbes, "more than half of Americans (54%) report having a side hustle at some point to generate extra money, pulling in $8,794, on average per year." Read this for more details: https://tinyurl.com/gigeconomystat1

Having said that, keep in mind that in practice, I have seen many people exceed this figure and make even more than that per month. The point I want to make with this though, is that you should forget what everyone else is making and focus on your own goals and objectives. And don't start with a huge unrealistic goal. Start small and build from that. Set yourself a small realistic goal and once you achieve it, set the next one. For example, start by aiming to pay for a cup of coffee or a few cups of coffee per month. Achieve that and then plan your next goal. I do realize this sounds like a very "small" goal, but a) I don't see many people lining up to pay for your coffee lol and b) one of the reasons I see people frequently fail when chasing their dreams in the Gig Economy is that they set very ambitious unrealistic goals and when they don't quickly achieve them they get disappointed and desist.

One of the key factors in being successful in the Gig Economy is persistence. So take my advice and start with small realistic goals. And if you quickly achieve them, great, awesome. Keep doing that and keep raising the bar, eventually you will get to your destination. Trust me.

CHAPTER 5: SHOULD I QUIT MY JOB?

No, I don't think so. At least not initially, and at least not until the revenue from whatever you do in the Gig Economy equals or exceeds whatever you make in your day to day job and does so consistently for several months. Ideally a year at a minimum. But then again, why quit your job and lose one source of income when you can have two? Or like me, multiple sources of income. I wouldn't, I haven't and I don't intend to. So I won't recommend it to you either. But what you do is entirely up to you. You will have to make your own choices and you will need to learn to trust your instincts. Quitting your job is a very personal decision and whatever I think about it is irrelevant. At the end of the day, you need to do what makes you happy regardless of whether other people understand it or not.

I have many colleagues and friends in the Gig Economy who have quit their job. But I wouldn't say this is common practice. It comes down to individual choices, personal circumstances and context.

CHAPTER 6: HOW DO I GET STARTED?

Getting started in the Gig Economy is not as hard as you might think. Just follow these steps:

Step 1 - Choose

The first step is basically to choose what you want to focus on. And like I said before, this should relate to what you can do, what you're passionate about and where you think you can provide most value. But don't worry too much about this decision. It's ok to make mistakes. It's ok if you choose something and then decide it's not what you expected or hoped for. Whatever you do, you will learn from that experience. It will make you wiser, stronger, faster. In this book, I will include a lot of options that will allow you to reflect about what you will start with initially. And I say initially, because once you have tasted the Gig Economy & Beyond, and once you see that you can actually make money by doing something else other than your day to day job, you will likely want to expand your new business. You will likely want to explore other opportunities in this incredible economy and of course, that is only natural. I would too, and I have.

Step 2 - Explore

Once you've made your choice of what you want to do you should explore a bit about it before getting started. This will save you precious time and reduce the learn curve as you position yourself in the Gig Economy. You can learn from what others have done, what has helped them and what hasn't. You should also make time to explore what the opportunity or company itself provides, since a lot of these products or services generally have knowledge bases, quick reference guides, videos, etc. You should also read about them in sites like Quora and watch Youtube videos. So think of this second step as your Research or Due Diligence Step. But don't get me wrong, I don't intend to convey that you should spend a lot of time doing this. Spend some time, but not more than a month.

Step 3 - Start

Enroll, join, sign up or do whatever needs to be done to get started with any of the options covered later in the book. The process of getting started will vary for each product, company or service that you wish to be a part of. Each have their own rules, guidelines, business model, etc. But generally speaking, starting tends to be easy. The complexity is more around having the tenacity to persist when initially you don't see the results that perhaps you were expecting. Remember, getting started in the Gig Economy is a bit like riding a bicycle. You will stumble at first, probably fall a few times but eventually, with practice and over time, you will master the craft. So manage your own expectations. Don't set the bar too high when you're just starting up. Don't expect to make what you make on your day job from day one. Or did you forget what you where earning when you started of as an Intern? Perhaps you weren't even earning anything at all, but you did it for the experience so you could add it to your CV. Remember? This is not that different. But sometimes people are just unrealistic. Start and take it one step at a time. If you make $1 dollar the first month, great, it's a start. It's a dollar you didn't have before. So don't worry too much about your baseline, just start and whatever you make the first month, the second or the third (if you didn't make anything the first few months), well make that your baseline. Keep a record of it in an excel file so that you can track your progress and work your way up from that. And don't get me wrong about any of this, some people are super talented or just lucky and start making a lot of money from the get go, but I wouldn't say that is the majority of people and I wouldn't treat that as a general rule. I wouldn't have that expectation and I don't what you to have it either.

CHAPTER 7: OTHER THINGS TO KEEP IN MIND WHEN GETTING STARTED

Your Location

Most Gigs in the Gig Economy are global. Meaning they are available to anyone from any country in the world, but some are local, available to specific markets and countries. So if you're not sure whether one of your options is available in your country, reach out to them directly and ask. Or check their FAQs, Help or Knowledge Base where this might be covered. Most (if not all) websites, apps, etc. in the Gig Economy have a Contact Us section where you can reach out to them for questions if you have any.

Taxes

Making money in the Gig Economy doesn't mean you are exempt from tax. Generally speaking, in most countries you have to pay tax on income regardless of where it comes from. But of course, the amount, percentage, rules, etc. vary from country to country and sometimes from state to state or region to region. So my recommendation on this is don't make assumptions and check with your accountant. If you don't have one, Google it, ask others in your same location or find communities where this might be covered. But I can tell you this from experience, most entities in the Gig Economy will not solve this for you, since you are not in a employee-employer relationship with them and they will likely expect you to sort this out yourself. This of course if probably not too relevant when you're getting started given the amount will likely be low, but over time this will become increasingly important.

Investment

Some people think they need a lot of money to start a Gig in the Gig Economy. The reality is you don't. Most (if not all) the time, all you need is tools or resources you already have: a smartphone, internet, a computer and your brain. Some people of course will argue otherwise and imply that making up front investments will set you up for success. I will leave that decision to you, but as a businessman and someone who started from nothing and with nothing, I will say this: keep it simple, start small, use what you have, learn to be recursive and productive and over time increase your investment as your business grows. Your Gig is your business, your startup. Treat it as such. Invest if you feel you must. But remember, don't add unnecessary fixed costs, especially when getting started. And don't let anyone tell you need a Ferrari to get from Point A to B, you don't. You can also get there walking, on a bicycle, a skateboard or even a bus. Creativity is one of your most valuable assets, use it.

CHAPTER 8: THE TWO TYPES OF GIGS IN THE GIG ECONOMY

Even though there are a ton of different Gigs out there and ways for you to make money in the modern world, I would say that all of them fall in one of two categories, and even though this may seem trivial, it's actually quite important and I'll explain why I personally think one is better than the other. Not that I want to discredit the other one or necessarily imply that you should ignore it, but you should at least reflect about their differences.

Category 1: Passive

Things that fall under this category require your time and effort, but generally speaking, you make the big investment up front and then reap the benefits over time, indefinitely. You might still invest more time and effort to continuously improve or enhance what you have done, but you will have a lot more freedom on when and how you do that, and even if you didn't do it, you'll probably still generate revenue from what you originally created. Examples of this would be an Online Course or a Merchandise Shop. You would invest time and effort in the setup and building your content, but after you do it, you can sit back and relax and watch the dollars coming in. You can make money while you sleep, at any point in time, anywhere in the world. Gigs that fall under this category would not require you to be physically present anywhere and would not involve you doing something to get something in return on a regular basis. Like I said, the big investment comes up front. At the beginning.

Gigs that fall in the passive category are not bound by the physical limits of space and time, so you could, for example, be generating revenue at exactly the same time from two different locations in the world. Here's a real world example, say you published a book and somebody in Europe bought your book at the exact same time somebody else did in the U.S., you would be making revenue from the same content at the same time from two different locations. And this could be occurring in different time zones while you were sleeping or watching TV. Like I explained before, the effort comes in at the beginning, when you spent the time to write the book. After it's done, it's done and you can regularly make money from it after it's published. This is a perfect example of a Gig that falls in this category.

Category 2: Transactional

Gigs that fall under this category require your time and effort on a regular basis to generate revenue. And they tend to be more transactional and a one off type of Gig. If you don't transact, then you don't get paid. Examples of this would be things like Uber or Taskrabbit. If you don't go out and drive or you don't go out and perform a task you don't get paid and because of the nature of these Gigs, they are bound by the physical limits of time and space, how much you can actually take on and how much you can actually do during a particular period of time because you are still, only human and there's only so much you can do, no matter how good or fast you are. And note this applies to both the digital and physical world, because even if you're working on a task remotely in the cloud, you still need to perform the task and it still requires time.

These second category is huge. It's probably bigger than the first one. And it probably requires less effort and investment, but it is also the one with less potential. So I would recommend you focus on Gigs that fall under the Passive Category, but again, that is up to you. There's nothing wrong with working on Gigs that are transactional in nature and of course that doesn't mean you can't make good money from them. You can.

In the following Chapters of this book we will cover different options to explore in the Gig Economy. They will include examples of both passive and transactional options and will allow to explore different opportunities.

CHAPTER 9: ONLINE COURSE CREATION (TEACHING) | PASSIVE

Online course creation is about sharing knowledge. Hence, this type of gig is also considered part of what is known as the knowledge economy (another name frequently given to the Gig Economy). Creating online courses is basically about you creating content for others to learn something. So this is a gig in which you are the producer, the teacher, the instructor, the author. And you can do as much or as little as you want in this regard by either doing most or all of the work yourself (recording, editing, marketing, etc.) or outsourcing it to others.

Key skills needed for online course creation include but are not limited to video production, video editing, audio production, audio editing, design, curriculum design, etc. But probably the most important aspect of any is you having knowledge about something which you can share with others. And if you are an expert in the field, that will play to your advantage.

With this Gig, like with many others, you don't really need prior experience in creating online courses. Even if you have never done it before you can still learn how to do it by leveraging on the tools and resources many of the online learning platforms provide. You can also take an online course yourself (and there are many free ones in case you're wondering), or you can do simple things like watching YouTube videos about it, read articles, blog posts or even books about online course creation. And of course, perhaps you can also read from other people who went through the same process, people who are current online teachers who one day weren't. You'll find that a lot of them have shared their experience online and there's a lot you can learn from that to make your learn curve shorter.

Below a list of platforms you can use to create, publish and commercialize your courses:

Udemy
https://www.udemy.com/teaching/?ref=teach_header

Note: They generally distribute over $100 Million in payments per year to Instructors, based on internal stats they shared at one of their live events.

Skillshare
https://www.skillshare.com/teach

StackSkills
https://stackskills.com/p/instructor-form

LinkedIn Learning
https://learning.linkedin.com/instructors

Pluralsight
https://www.pluralsight.com/teach

Envato Tuts+
https://tutsplus.com/teach

Packtpub
https://www.packtpub.com/contact/

Here's an example of how I have done this:
https://www.udemy.com/user/_mauriciorubio/

CHAPTER 10: WRITING & SELLING BOOKS | PASSIVE

In the old days you would write a book and someone else would publish it, distribute it and commercialise it. In the modern world of the Gig Economy and Beyond you can do all of this yourself but most importantly, you can self publish your book in less than ten minutes. Literally it is that easy. I did it myself, when I published this book you're reading right now. Anyone can do it. No special skills required. The "hard" part is having everything ready for publication, mainly the book which you can write on a Word document. Now writing a book does take time, but keep in mind there are no hard rules on this. You can write a 20-page book or a thousand page novel. The subject, style, length, etc. is entirely up to you. And one of my favorite things about this is, you can update the book whenever you like as many times as you like. So keep it simple and don't over think it. You can always make changes to it later if you like.

The King in self publication is KDP (Kindle Direct Publishing) from Amazon, and they have a fund of over $20 Million dollars they distribute monthly among authors who are part of their Kindle Select program. In a Nutshell you get a piece of the pie based on the number of pages readers read from your books every month, the more pages they read, the more money you make. It's a simple formula. And we're not talking peanuts here by the way, as I mentioned before, the money distributed generally exceeds $20 Million per month! Now of course what you get from that will depend on the popularity of your books, but needless to say if they're good, many people will read them and more people reading them will translate into more revenue. Here's the beauty of this fund from Amazon's Kindle Select program, if you're part of it that is extra and additional to sales from your book, both digital and physical.

Now of course Amazon isn't the only option, but it's probably the best one. But here are the main options for you to explore:

Amazon
https://kdp.amazon.com/en_US/

Note: As per their own website, they distribute over $20 Million per month among authors who are part of the Kindle Select program.

Lulu
http://www.lulu.com/sell

BookBaby
https://www.bookbaby.com/

Blurb
https://www.blurb.com/sell-and-distribute

Leanpub
https://leanpub.com/authors

The Book Patch
https://www.thebookpatch.com/

Here's an example of how I have done this:
https://www.amazon.com/Mauricio-Rubio/e/B07WYZQMLW

CHAPTER 11: DOING TASKS FOR OTHERS | TRANSACTIONAL

This is probably one of the most common (if not the most common) of all Gigs in the Gig Economy and it's probably where it all started. Not that this didn't exist before, because it did, but it didn't exist in the way it does today in which you can do tasks for anyone in the world from anywhere in the world. And you can of course, still do local tasks as well if you happen to be in the same location where the task is required. And jobs for both scenarios abound.

Doing tasks for other people involves pretty much any type of skill or job you can think of. But, that doesn't mean you need to have skills or talents across all fields or categories, it just means there's a ton of options for you to choose from.

Given the nature of Gigs that fall in this group, building an online profile with great reviews and a great reputation will become increasingly important and will help you succeed. But don't worry too much if you don't have one to start with, that's ok, and at some point nobody had one. Everyone had to start at the beginning, with zero experience and zero reviews. Building a profile and a reputation takes time, but don't over think it and don't worry too much about the future. Just get started and see how you go. You might end up falling in love with Gigs in this group and decide like many, to focus solely on this.

If you're wondering what types of jobs you can find on these platforms, like I said before, pretty much anything you can think of. From tasks as wide and broad as assembling furniture, cleaning, data entry, voice overs, translations, marketing, project management and interview preparation to pretty much anything else you can think of.

Fiverr
https://www.fiverr.com/start_selling

Freelancer
https://www.freelancer.com/

Upwork

https://www.upwork.com/

Guru

https://www.guru.com/

TaskRabbit

https://www.taskrabbit.com/become-a-tasker?source=homepage-get-started

Airtasker

https://www.airtasker.com/earn-money/

Hello Alfred

https://www.helloalfred.com/alfreds/

Cavalry

https://www.cavalryfreelancing.com/freelancer/

CHAPTER 12: SELLING DIGITAL ASSETS | PASSIVE

In the world of the Gig Economy and Beyond having digital skills is definitely a plus, since there are multiple and unlimited ways for you to make money. Especially if you have creative talents in fields such as photography, design and development. If you do, you should explore the following options:

Envato
https://author.envato.com/

Getty Images
https://www.gettyimages.com.au/workwithus#

Foap
https://www.foap.com/photographer

CHAPTER 13: DELIVERING FOOD | TRANSACTIONAL

Unless you're living under a rock in the modern world, you've probably used a food delivery service. And even though we have grown accustomed to having this around, two decades ago, this didn't exist. It wasn't around, it wasn't an option. Yet now, it is. Not only for you the customer or consumer receiving the food but also for those who want to provide it, specifically to deliver it.

There are now more and more Gigs across different countries expanding in this booming field. And it is a growing field just so you know as a consequence of one of the side effects of living in a hyper connected world: people are always busy or distracted and they have less time. People value convenience and are more than willing to pay for it. Hence why every month or every few months a new player enters this field somewhere in the world.

So if you would like to explore this Gig, here are a few options:

UberEats
https://www.uber.com/au/en/drive/delivery/

Deliveroo
https://deliveroo.co.uk/apply

Note: They claim you can make as much as £120 a day.

Doordash
https://www.doordash.com/dasher/signup/

Postmates
https://fleet.postmates.com/

Caviar
https://www.trycaviar.com/apply

Note: They claim you can earn up to $25/hour

Grubhub

https://driver.grubhub.com/

Bite Squad

https://www.bitesquad.com/apply

Note: They claim you can make up to $20/hour

Waitr

https://waitrapp.com/careers/driver

Note: They claim you can earn on average $13–$17/hour and keep 100% of your tips.

CHAPTER 14: SELL YOUR MERCHANDISE | PASSIVE

One of the things I find most amazing of the modern world is the ability everyone has to create so much with so little. Like for example, and online shop to sell merchandise, with only a computer, the internet and their creative mind. Isn't that awesome? Seriously it is. I mean, I still remember a time when such a concept didn't even exist. Yet now it's so easy! I setup my own merchandise shop in only a few minutes, so I can definitely speak from experience about how easy it is.

Selling merchandise is about selling t-shirts, mugs, hoodies and stuff like that. You can pick your own products, prices, colors and which company to use to setup your own shop. One of my favorite things about this is that there are already a ton of well positioned market places out there where you can just place your products for free! So no setup costs, no creation costs, nothing. You just add and they take a percentage of the sale when a sale is made. So you never lose money. And best of all you don't even need to have any creative talents yourself. You can always use one of the free designs from a site like Unsplash to place on your merchandise or you can hire a Designer to create one for you. But, remember, try to keep your costs to zero or to a minimum when getting started. Don't invest too much when you're not making any money, that's one of the best tips I can give you.

Spreadshop
https://www.spreadshop.com/

Printful
https://www.printful.com/

Printify
https://printify.com/

Redbubble
https://www.redbubble.com/about/selling

Merch by Amazon
https://merch.amazon.com/

Etsy

https://www.etsy.com/sell?ref=ftr

And here's my own shop in case you were wondering about it:

https://shop.spreadshirt.com/mauriciorubio

CHAPTER 15: PODCASTING & VOICE OVERS | PASSIVE

Podcasting and doing voice overs used to be for professionals. Nowadays, it's for everyone, anyone can do it. And you don't need to much to get started. Mainly a mobile phone and your voice, that's it. And of course the confidence and willingness of getting started.

One of the things I really like about this is that unlike many of the other Gigs, this one is probably one I would say it's quite easy and quick to do. Especially if you're going raw and not doing too much editing. Of course that might seem "unprofessional" to some, but you don't need to be super professional to get started. As a matter of fact, there's not a lot of quality assurance on this, so how much editing you do, pretty much is on you really. And like I said before, many people are doing this just with their smartphone. You don't really need more than that, but like anything else you can get as sophisticated as you like. Not that there's anything wrong with that of course.

Some people laugh when I say, there's a lot of money in Podcasting, and trust me when I say there is, there is. It's huge and it is also a growing field. Particularly as more and more people discover that anyone can do it and that it's a lot of fun. I project this Gig will continue to grow massively. You can see this in things such as sales of Apple's Airpods and smart wearables surpassing those of Iphones and in seeing things such as people listening more and more to Podcasts when commuting to and from work, while working out at the gym or while driving. That trend will only continue to increase. But if you still doubt me, here's another stat for you which showcases how this Podcast makes over $50 Thousand dollars a month: https://tinyurl.com/gigeconomystat2

Aside from what I mentioned above, there are also tons of opportunities in doing voice overs for others in things such as audio books, commercials and so forth. Below are some of the options you can explore if you're interested in the Gigs covered in this chapter:

Anchor

https://anchor.fm/

ACX

https://www.acx.com/help/narrators/200484550

Podbean

https://www.podbean.com/

Whooshkaa

https://www.whooshkaa.com/

Blubrry

https://create.blubrry.com/resources/blubrry-affiliate-program/

Here's an example of how I do this:

https://podcasts.apple.com/us/podcast/join-me-for-coffee/id1291735010?mt=2

CHAPTER 16: MICRO-INVESTING | PASSIVE

This is one I really like because of it's simplicity and set and forget nature. Micro-investing as the name implies, it about investing small amounts of money to create and generate more money. So in essence, it helps you grow your money and make more money as well (return on investment and re-investment).

In the modern world of the Gig Economy and Beyond, you can use technology at your finger tips and the power of compounding to generate more money from your own money. But best of all these tools allow you to do this hassle free and without needing to make heavy investments or waiting on having a huge deposit.

The concept works like this: let's say you go an buy a cup of coffee and it costs $3.5 dollars. The app or system can round this app to $4, and use that extra 50 cents to invest your money to in turn generate more money for you in the future. I know, right now as you're reading this, you're probably thinking that is too small. Well, trust me when I say that over time that is not small at all. Everyone spends money. Everyone, but few micro-invest. Those that do, stay ahead. I do this and have done this for years now and have amassed a substantial amount of money. Here are the options you can explore:

Acorns
https://www.acorns.com/

Raiz
https://raizinvest.com.au/

Stash
https://www.stashinvest.com/

www.ingramcontent.com/pod-product-compliance
Lightning Source LLC
Chambersburg PA
CBHW030535220526
45463CB00007B/2852